BIRDERS' 1998
Engagement Calendar

ISBN 1-55209-680-7

A FIREFLY BOOK

Published by
Firefly Books Ltd.
3680 Victoria Park Avenue
Willowdale, Ontario
Canada M2H 3K1

Design by Janice McLean

Produced by
Bookmakers Press Inc.
12 Pine Street
Kingston, Ontario
K7K 1W1

Printed and bound in Canada by
Friesens
Altona, Manitoba

Front cover: **American Avocet** (*Recurvirostra americana*). Among the hand-somest of the shorebirds, the American avocet is readily identified by the long recurved bill that is one of its most distinctive features. The avocet commonly nests in the Great Basin region and grasslands of the West. There, it feeds on small aquatic invertebrates and the seeds of marsh plants, which it sieves out as it systematically sweeps its bill back and forth through the water.

Back cover: **Yellow Warbler** (*Dendroica petechia*)

BIRDERS' 1998
Engagement Calendar

Photographs by Wayne Lynch

FIREFLY BOOKS

December/January

Bird Sightings

28 Sunday

29 Monday

30 Tuesday

31 Wednesday

1 Thursday
New Year's Day

2 Friday

3 Saturday

llow-Bellied Sapsucker (*Sphyrapicus varius*). This female
ow-bellied sapsucker is carrying a mouthful of carpenter ants to her nestlings
tree cavity. A protein-rich diet such as this is necessary for the normal
vth of the youngsters. Adult birds drill rows of shallow holes in the bark of
s and drink the sap. The sapsucker is a common woodpecker throughout
leciduous forests of North America.

DECEMBER 1997

	1	2	3	4	5	6
7	8	9	10	11	12	13
14	15	16	17	18	19	20
21	22	23	24	25	26	27
28	29	30	31			

JANUARY

				1	2	3
4	5	6	7	8	9	10
11	12	13	14	15	16	17
18	19	20	21	22	23	24
25	26	27	28	29	30	31

Bird Sightings

4 Sunday

5 Monday

6 Tuesday

7 Wednesday

8 Thursday

9 Friday

0 Saturday

olden Eagle (*Aquila chrysaetos*). The golden eagle has a wide
:ibution in North America and Eurasia in remote mountains, grasslands
deserts. Like many birds of prey, the eagle uses a threat display, called
ntling," to deter other eagles from stealing its prey. A mantling eagle raises
feathers on its head and neck, partly opens its wings and sits back on its
freeing its powerful taloned feet to strike forward.

JANUARY						
				1	2	3
4	5	6	7	8	9	10
11	12	13	14	15	16	17
18	19	20	21	22	23	24
25	26	27	28	29	30	31

anuary

11 Sunday

12 Monday

13 Tuesday

14 Wednesday

15 Thursday

16 Friday

17 Saturday

ranklin's Gull (*Larus pipixcan*). The Franklin's gull nests on an :hored mass of vegetation in cattail and bulrush marshes throughout the itral Great Plains of North America. They gather in large, noisy colonies—as ny as 20,000 birds have been reported in a single colony. This gull eats mainly ects and makes a habit of following farmers plowing their fields to snatch up grubs and cutworms that are unearthed.

JANUARY						
				1	2	3
4	5	6	7	8	9	10
11	12	13	14	15	16	17
18	19	20	21	22	23	24
25	26	27	28	29	30	31

Bird Sightings

18 Sunday

19 Monday
Martin Luther King Day (U.S.)

20 Tuesday

21 Wednesday

22 Thursday

23 Friday

24 Saturday

merican White Pelican (*Pelecanus erythrorhynchos*). Twenty-
years ago, there were fewer than an estimated 16,000 breeding pairs of
erican white pelicans left in the birds' nesting range in central North America.
day, there are more than 50,000 pairs, and the bird has been removed from
threatened-species list. These large fish-eating water birds nest in colonies,
ically on low, bare islands in the middle of large lakes, safe from predators.

JANUARY

				1	2	3
4	5	6	7	8	9	10
11	12	13	14	15	16	17
18	19	20	21	22	23	24
25	26	27	28	29	30	31

anuary

25 Sunday

26 Monday

27 Tuesday

28 Wednesday

29 Thursday

30 Friday

31 Saturday

reat Horned Owl (*Bubo virginianus*). The great horned owl is
nd from Canada's northern tree line to the windswept plains of Patagonia, at
southern tip of South America. Occupying an amazing diversity of habitats—
n coniferous forests and cactus deserts to paramos and tropical rainforests
e owl eats virtually anything it can subdue, including small mammals, birds
reptiles. This young owl has left the nest but is still being fed by its parents.

JANUARY						
				1	2	3
4	5	6	7	8	9	10
11	12	13	14	15	16	17
18	19	20	21	22	23	24
25	26	27	28	29	30	31

ebruary

1 Sunday

2 Monday
Groundhog Day

3 Tuesday

4 W

5 Thursday

6 Friday

7 Saturday

:arlet Tanager (*Piranga olivacea*). The male scarlet tanager is one he most colorful songbirds of the deciduous forests and mixed woodlands of :ern North America. But on its wintering grounds in South America, the showy e resembles the female, with dull green plumage above, straw-yellow coloring w and dark wings. The scarlet tanager forages from the ground to the tree-s, searching for ants, aphids, caterpillars, cicadas, worms, spiders and snails.

FEBRUARY						
1	2	3	4	5	6	7
8	9	10	11	12	13	14
15	16	17	18	19	20	21
22	23	24	25	26	27	28

February

8 Sunday

9 Monday

10 Tuesday

11 Wednesday

12 Thursday

13 Friday

14 Saturday
Valentine's Day

---

merican Coot (*Fulica americana*). A cautious American coot nbs onto its floating cattail nest in a marsh in western Canada, where it is ubating 11 buff-colored eggs. The coot is one of the most successful members he rail family and lives in wetlands from southern Canada to central South erica. It feeds on aquatic plants, invertebrates and small fish by tipping up a duck or making shallow dives.

FEBRUARY						
1	2	3	4	5	6	7
8	9	10	11	12	13	14
15	16	17	18	19	20	21
22	23	24	25	26	27	28

February

15 Sunday

16 Monday
Heritage Day (Canada)
Presidents' Day (U.S.)

17 Tuesday

18 Wednesday

19 Thursday

20 Friday

21 Saturday

Gray Jay (*Perisoreus canadensis*). The gray jay is a year-round resident of northern and western coniferous forests of North America and is a common scavenger at animal carcasses. Nesting in February and March, this jay is one of the earliest birds to lay eggs each spring. It is no coincidence that the gray jay's nesting season occurs at the same time that many animals succumb to the rigors of winter and carcasses are plentiful.

FEBRUARY						
1	2	3	4	5	6	7
8	9	10	11	12	13	14
15	16	17	18	19	20	21
22	23	24	25	26	27	28

February

Bird Sightings

22 Sunday

23 Monday

24 Tuesday

25 Wednesday
Ash Wednesday

26 Thursday

27 Friday

28 Saturday

rakeet Auklet (*Cyclorrhynchus psittacula*). The parakeet auklet
ngs to the auk family, the northern hemisphere's counterpart to the south-
hemisphere's penguin. With its parrotlike beak, the auklet might seem more
ome in the tropical rainforest than in the cold subarctic waters of the North
ic, where it resides. The bird feeds on marine invertebrates and nests in
ces in rocky shorelines and sea cliffs.

FEBRUARY

1	2	3	4	5	6	7
8	9	10	11	12	13	14
15	16	17	18	19	20	21
22	23	24	25	26	27	28

1 Sunday

2 Monday

3 Tuesday

4 Wednesday

5 Thursday

6 Friday

7 Saturday

naparte's Gull (*Larus philadelphia*). When an intruder is near est, the Bonaparte's gull perches nearby and noisily screams its displeasure. ke most gulls that nest on the ground or on cliff ledges, this one builds a of twigs and sticks in a tree near water. The Bonaparte's gull breeds through-he central and western spruce-fir forests of northern North America and ers along both coastlines of the southern United States.

MARCH						
1	2	3	4	5	6	7
8	9	10	11	12	13	14
15	16	17	18	19	20	21
22	23	24	25	26	27	28
29	30	31				

Bird Sightings

8 Sunday

9 Monday

10 Tuesday

11 Wednesday

12 Thursday
Purim

13 Friday

14 Saturday

ectacled Eider (*Somateria fischeri*). A large white area edged with
n black line surrounds the eider's eyes and accounts for its common name;
pattern is far less dramatic in the female. Limited to the coastlines of the
ng Sea, northern Alaska and northeastern Siberia, the spectacled eider has
smallest breeding range of the four eider species. This large diving sea duck
a strong, broad bill that it uses to crush mussels, the main food in its diet.

MARCH						
1	2	3	4	5	6	7
8	9	10	11	12	13	14
15	16	17	18	19	20	21
22	23	24	25	26	27	28
29	30	31				

March

15 Sunday

16 Monday

17 Tuesday
St. Patrick's Day

18 Wednesday

19 Thursday

20 Friday
Vernal Equinox

21 Saturday

orthern Cardinal (*Cardinalis cardinalis*). The size and shape
bird's bill are determined principally by the food it eats. The stout bill of the
thern cardinal is well adapted to crack tough seeds, although the bird also
grasshoppers, termites, caterpillars, 51 kinds of beetles and 33 types of wild
s. The cardinal is a year-round resident of woodlands, streamside thickets
urban gardens in the eastern United States and Mexico.

MARCH

1	2	3	4	5	6	7
8	9	10	11	12	13	14
15	16	17	18	19	20	21
22	23	24	25	26	27	28
29	30	31				

Bird Sightings

22 Sunday

23 Monday

24 Tuesday

25 Wednesday

26 Thursday

27 Friday

28 Saturday

ountain Bluebird (*Sialia currucoides*). The iridescent male
ntain bluebird is a popular breeding bird throughout the rangelands and
dows of the West, usually at elevations above 5,000 feet. The bluebird nests
d woodpecker holes, cavities in rock piles, holes in stumps and nest boxes.
n it flies to its nest, a bluebird invariably lands on a nearby perch to check
anger before disappearing inside.

MARCH						
1	2	3	4	5	6	7
8	9	10	11	12	13	14
15	16	17	18	19	20	21
22	23	24	25	26	27	28
29	30	31				

March/April

29 Sunday

30 Monday

31 Tuesday

1 Wednesday

2 Thursday

3 Friday

4 Saturday

MARCH

1	2	3	4	5	6	7
8	9	10	11	12	13	14
15	16	17	18	19	20	21
22	23	24	25	26	27	28
29	30	31				

ɔrned Grebe (*Podiceps auritus*). The horned grebe feeds, sleeps, ts and nests on the water, carrying its downy young on its back. Even when dult bird dives underwater to search for a meal of invertebrates or fish, the ɡ grebes stay aboard, safely tucked under the parent's wings. Horned grebes on freshwater lakes and ponds throughout Canada and the northwestern ed States as well as all across Russia and Scandinavia.

APRIL

				1	2	3	4
5	6	7	8	9	10	11
12	13	14	15	16	17	18
19	20	21	22	23	24	25
26	27	28	29	30		

April

5 Sunday
Palm Sunday
Daylight Saving Time Begins

6 Monday

7 Tuesday

8 Wednesday

9 Thursday

0 Friday
Good Friday

1 Saturday
First Day of Passover

ng Penguin (*Aptenodytes patagonicus*). It is easy to understand why late Roger Tory Peterson, the famed bird illustrator, called the king penguin favorite bird in his favorite family of birds." Although this handsome penguin ins adult size and coloration by 3 years of age, it may not breed until it is 6 or he king penguin, which lives on remote islands in the Subantarctic, is a deep r that hunts squid and lanternfish at depths of up to 780 feet.

APRIL						
		1	2	3	4
5	6	7	8	9	10	11
12	13	14	15	16	17	18
19	20	21	22	23	24	25
26	27	28	29	30		

April

2 Sunday
Easter Sunday

3 Monday

4 Tuesday

5 Wednesday

6 Thursday

7 Friday

8 Saturday

---

ge Grouse (*Centrocercus urophasianus*). The importance of sage in winter diet of the sage grouse earned the bird its common name. The largest ìber of the grouse family in North America, the sage grouse is restricted to sagebrush flats and shortgrass prairies of the central Great Plains. For several ìths each spring, males gather in groups of up to 50 birds or more to strut perform for prospective mates.

APRIL						
				1	2	3	4
5	6	7	8	9	10	11
12	13	14	15	16	17	18
19	20	21	22	23	24	25
26	27	28	29	30		

April

Bird Sightings

19 Sunday

20 Monday

21 Tuesday

22 Wednesday
Earth Day

23 Thursday

24 Friday

25 Saturday

---

ack-Crowned Night-Heron (*Nycticorax nycticorax*).
black-crowned night-heron was photographed in the Falkland Islands some
miles from the tip of South America. The wandering spirit of this medium-
l heron has enabled it to colonize much of the world, including North, Central
South America, Europe, Africa and southern Asia. Its large eyes are an adapta-
to nocturnal foraging for amphibians, reptiles, mollusks, leeches and fish.

APRIL			
1	2	3	4
5 6 7 8	9 10 11		
12 13 14 15	16 17 18		
19 20 21 22	23 24 25		
26 27 28 29 30			

April/May

Bird Sightings

26 Sunday

_____

_____

27 Monday

_____

_____

28 Tuesday

_____

_____

29 Wednesday

_____

_____

30 Thursday

_____

_____

1 Friday

_____

_____

		APRIL				
			1	2	3	4
5	6	7	8	9	10	11
12	13	14	15	16	17	18
19	20	21	22	23	24	25
26	27	28	29	30		

2 Saturday

ommon Loon (_Gavia immer_). This loon is found in remote lakes oreal forests all across North America—where its cry has become a symbol ne northern wilderness—and along the southern coastline of Greenland. In ope, the common name for this bird is the great northern diver, a reflection ne loon's underwater capabilities. The loon dives for fish and invertebrates orays that last up to 60 seconds and reach depths of 200 feet.

		MAY				
					1	2
3	4	5	6	7	8	9
10	11	12	13	14	15	16
17	18	19	20	21	22	23
24/31	25	26	27	28	29	30

May

Bird Sightings

3 Sunday

4 Monday

5 Tuesday

6 Wednesday

7 Thursday

8 Friday

9 Saturday

reat **Blue Heron** (*Ardea herodias*). The bulky stick nest of the
.t blue heron may be built on rock ledges and sea cliffs, but most often, it is
.ted in trees up to 90 feet off the ground. Typically, the heron is a sit-and-
.e hunter, standing motionless in the water waiting for prey to come within
.e. It eats insects, fish, rodents, frogs, lizards and snakes, even venomous
.s. The heron is found in wetlands from southern Canada to Central America.

MAY						
					1	2
3	4	5	6	7	8	9
10	11	12	13	14	15	16
17	18	19	20	21	22	23
24/31	25	26	27	28	29	30

May

Bird Sightings

10 Sunday
Mother's Day

11 Monday

12 Tuesday

13 Wednesday

14 Thursday

15 Friday

16 Saturday

sprey (*Pandion haliaetus*). The osprey is one of the most cosmopolitan
s of prey, inhabiting the freshwater and saltwater areas of every continent
ept Antarctica. Shown here with a large catfish, the hook-billed osprey is a
cialist, preying almost exclusively on fish. Typically, the bird grasps the fish
n the surface of the water, but it may occasionally disappear in a feet-first dive
leaves only its wingtips visible above the water.

		MAY				
					1	2
3	4	5	6	7	8	9
10	11	12	13	14	15	16
17	18	19	20	21	22	23
24/31	25	26	27	28	29	30

May

Bird Sightings

17 Sunday

18 Monday
Victoria Day (Canada)

19 Tuesday

20 Wednesday

21 Thursday

22 Friday

23 Saturday

---

ing Eider (*Somateria spectabilis*). The male king eider is easily the st brightly colored duck anywhere in the bird's vast circumpolar arctic range, e the female king eider is completely brown-colored. The female incubates eggs alone in a down-lined nest on the ground, partly shielded by rocks or etation, sometimes a quarter of a mile from water. She may not eat for the re 23 days that she is sitting on the eggs.

MAY						
					1	2
3	4	5	6	7	8	9
10	11	12	13	14	15	16
17	18	19	20	21	22	23
24/31	25	26	27	28	29	30

May

24 Sunday

25 Monday
Memorial Day (U.S.)

26 Tuesday

27 Wednesday

28 Thursday

29 Friday

30 Saturday

orthern Saw-Whet Owl (*Aegolius acadicus*). The bright-
:d northern saw-whet owl is just eight inches tall. Relatively common throughout
forests, swamps and bogs of North America, the saw-whet's small size and secre-
nocturnal nature keep it hidden from most people. For a few weeks during the
ng breeding season, its repeated single-note whistle may be the only clue to its
sence. This elusive little hunter preys mostly on insects and small rodents.

MAY						
					1	2
3	4	5	6	7	8	9
10	11	12	13	14	15	16
17	18	19	20	21	22	23
24/31	25	26	27	28	29	30

May/June

31 Sunday

1 Monday

2 Tuesday

3 Wednesday

4 Thursday

5 Friday

MAY						
					1	2
3	4	5	6	7	8	9
10	11	12	13	14	15	16
17	18	19	20	21	22	23
24/31	25	26	27	28	29	30

6 Saturday

la Woodpecker (*Melanerpes uropygialis*). This gila woodpecker
es the blossom of a prickly pear cactus in search of beetles. Gila woodpeck-
at a variety of foods, ranging from bird eggs and insects to berries and cactus
s. In the cactus deserts of the American Southwest and northwestern Mexico,
r chattering calls are a familiar sound. These handsome birds excavate nest
s up to 19 inches deep in the large pulpy trunks of saguaro cacti.

JUNE						
1	2	3	4	5	6	
7	8	9	10	11	12	13
14	15	16	17	18	19	20
21	22	23	24	25	26	27
28	29	30				

une

7 Sunday

_____

_____

8 Monday

_____

_____

9 Tuesday

_____

_____

0 Wednesday

_____

_____

1 Thursday

_____

_____

2 Friday

_____

_____

3 Saturday

_____

_____

---

oland Sandpiper (_Bartramia longicauda_). When alighting, the nd sandpiper holds its wings above its back for a few seconds before folding n. In spring and summer, the bird is found in the fields and rolling pastures of central Great Plains of North America. Like so many different birds of the tree-prairies, the male upland sandpiper sings on the wing while circling high in the On the ground, it forages for anything small that scuttles through the grass.

JUNE					
1	2	3	4	5	6
7	8	9	10	11	12	13
14	15	16	17	18	19	20
21	22	23	24	25	26	27
28	29	30				

Bird Sightings

4 Sunday

5 Monday

6 Tuesday

7 Wednesday

8 Thursday

9 Friday

0 Saturday

ld Eagle (*Haliaeetus leucocephalus*). The characteristic white head
nage of the bald eagle is acquired when adults are 4 to 5 years of age. This
e bird of prey ranges along much of the North American coastline and
ughout the continent's northern forests wherever there are large lakes.
ough the powerful eagle feeds largely on fish, it may also hunt seabirds,
krats, rabbits, squirrels and even young sea otters.

JUNE					
1	2	3	4	5	6
7	8	9	10	11	12	13
14	15	16	17	18	19	20
21	22	23	24	25	26	27
28	29	30				

June

21 Sunday
Father's Day
Summer Solstice

22 Monday

23 Tuesday

24 Wednesday
Saint-Jean-Baptiste (Québec)

25 Thursday

26 Friday

27 Saturday

bine's Gull (*Xema sabini*). As with all gulls, the fork-tailed male female Sabine's gulls are identical in appearance and share the incubation e eggs. They often nest in association with arctic terns, which, like the gulls, essively defend their nests against predators. In this way, the two birds fit from each other's pugnaciousness. The gulls hunt for small fish and aceans on the ocean and tundra lakes.

JUNE					
1	2	3	4	5	6
7	8	9	10	11	12	13
14	15	16	17	18	19	20
21	22	23	24	25	26	27
28	29	30				

ne/July

28 Sunday

29 Monday

30 Tuesday

1 Wednesday
Canada Day (Canada)

2 Thursday

3 Friday

4 Saturday
Independence Day (U.S.)

nbu Fruit-Dove (*Ptilinopus jambu*). The pink breast patch
tifies this bird as a male jambu fruit-dove; the female has a green chest.
jambu fruit-dove usually travels alone, searching the lowland rainforests and
grove swamps of the Malay Peninsula for fruiting trees. Despite its colorful
age, the fruit-dove may be easily overlooked, because it is a secretive bird
spends much of its time perched motionless on a forest branch.

JUNE					
1	2	3	4	5	6
7	8	9	10	11	12	13
14	15	16	17	18	19	20
21	22	23	24	25	26	27
28	29	30			

JULY						
		1	2	3	4
5	6	7	8	9	10	11
12	13	14	15	16	17	18
19	20	21	22	23	24	25
26	27	28	29	30	31

ıly

5 Sunday

6 Monday

7 Tuesday

8 Wednesday

9 Thursday

0 Friday

1 Saturday

owy **Egret** (*Egretta thula*). The long, delicate plumes on the head, and back of this snowy egret are part of the bird's courtship plumage. A ıry ago, hundreds of thousands of egrets were shamelessly slaughtered for feathers, which were used to trim women's hats. Today, egret numbers recovered, and the birds are now common in wetlands from the southern :d States to southern South America.

JULY						
			1	2	3	4
5	6	7	8	9	10	11
12	13	14	15	16	17	18
19	20	21	22	23	24	25
26	27	28	29	30	31	

July

2 Sunday

3 Monday

4 Tuesday

5 Wednesday

6 Thursday

7 Friday

8 Saturday

ιe Grouse (*Dendragapus obscurus*). Male blue grouse hoot and
e colorful throat pouches in showy displays during the spring breeding
on. These birds range throughout the deciduous and coniferous forests of
estern mountains and coastal regions of North America. While the grouse
s a diet of berries, insects, flowers and leaf buds, it also eats resinous
er needles, a food distasteful to most other birds.

		JULY				
			1	2	3	4
5	6	7	8	9	10	11
12	13	14	15	16	17	18
19	20	21	22	23	24	25
26	27	28	29	30	31	

ıly

Bird Sightings

9 Sunday

0 Monday

1 Tuesday

2 Wednesday

3 Thursday

4 Friday

5 Saturday

low Warbler (*Dendroica petechia*). Found from the Atlantic
ı to the Pacific and from the Arctic to Mexico, the yellow warbler has the
t range of any warbler in North America. The red-streaked male advertises
wnership of a small nesting territory by singing from half a dozen exposed
such as the one pictured here. The warbler preys on caterpillars as well as
ːs, beetles and grasshoppers.

JULY						
			1	2	3	4
5	6	7	8	9	10	11
12	13	14	15	16	17	18
19	20	21	22	23	24	25
26	27	28	29	30	31	

ıly/August

Bird Sightings

6 Sunday

7 Monday

8 Tuesday

9 Wednesday

0 Thursday

1 Friday

1 Saturday

JULY

				1	2	3	4
5	6	7	8	9	10	11
12	13	14	15	16	17	18
19	20	21	22	23	24	25
26	27	28	29	30	31

nada Goose (*Branta canadensis*). The Canada goose is found ıghout the continent and is the most widespread goose in North America. nany people, the honking V-shaped flocks of Canada geese winging over- in spring or autumn are a sign of seasonal transition. Like all waterfowl, anada goose may oil and clean its feathers over a dozen times a day to tain their insulative and waterproof qualities.

AUGUST

						1
2	3	4	5	6	7	8
9	10	11	12	13	14	15
16	17	18	19	20	21	22
23/30	24/31	25	26	27	28	29

ugust

Bird Sightings

2 Sunday

3 Monday
Civic Holiday (Canada)

4 Tuesday

5 Wednesday

6 Thursday

7 Friday

8 Saturday

gnificent Frigatebird (*Fregata magnificens*). The magnifi-frigatebird is a bird of the Tropics, found on the warm Atlantic and Pacific s of the Americas. The agile frigatebird spends long hours soaring on its -foot wingspan, swooping down to pluck flying fish from the ocean's ce, but rarely landing on the water. This male frigatebird has inflated his oyant throat pouch in an attempt to lure a mate to his side.

AUGUST

						1
2	3	4	5	6	7	8
9	10	11	12	13	14	15
16	17	18	19	20	21	22
23/30	24/31	25	26	27	28	29

ugust

9 Sunday

0 Monday

1 Tuesday

2 Wednesday

3 Thursday

4 Friday

5 Saturday

ainson's Hawk (*Buteo swainsoni*). The Swainson's hawk nests ees or bushes on the central Great Plains of North America and winters in pampas of Argentina, making an annual round trip of 15,000 miles—the est migration of any hawk on the continent. On its northern breeding nds, the hawk hunts mainly rodents, such as gophers and mice, while in ntina, it feeds on grasshoppers and other insects.

		AUGUST				
						1
2	3	4	5	6	7	8
9	10	11	12	13	14	15
16	17	18	19	20	21	22
23/30	24/31	25	26	27	28	29

ugust

16 Sunday

17 Monday

18 Tuesday

19 Wednesday

20 Thursday

21 Friday

22 Saturday

ue-Footed Booby (*Sula nebouxii*). The blue-footed booby und along the western tropical coastline of Central and South America, ɔugh the unwary female in this picture was photographed in the Galápagos ɪds. One subtle way to distinguish the female of this species of booby is to nine the eyes; the central part of the female's iris is pigmented black, so the appears to have a dilated pupil.

AUGUST

						1
2	3	4	5	6	7	8
9	10	11	12	13	14	15
16	17	18	19	20	21	22
23/30	24/31	25	26	27	28	29

Bird Sightings

23 Sunday

_____

24 Monday

_____

25 Tuesday

_____

26 Wednesday

_____

27 Thursday

_____

28 Friday

_____

29 Saturday

_____

ng-Necked Duck (*Aythya collaris*). The ring-necked duck ommon breeding bird in ponds, lakes and wetlands all across southern da and the northern United States. In winter, it migrates to Mexico and the ern-tier states. A diving duck that hunts underwater for snails and aquatic ts, it propels itself with large webbed feet positioned far back on its body, e they generate the greatest propulsion.

AUGUST

						1
2	3	4	5	6	7	8
9	10	11	12	13	14	15
16	17	18	19	20	21	22
23/30	24/31	25	26	27	28	29

0 Sunday

1 Monday

1 Tuesday

2 Wednesday

3 Thursday

4 Friday

5 Saturday

AUGUST						
						1
2	3	4	5	6	7	8
9	10	11	12	13	14	15
16	17	18	19	20	21	22
23/30	24/31	25	26	27	28	29

rrowing Owl (*Athene cunicularia*). The small 9-to-10-inch-tall owing owl is the principal owl of the treeless grasslands of North, Central South America. Its long, lightly feathered legs are an adaptation that enables iminutive bird to dissipate body heat. Unlike any other owl, it nests under- nd in a burrow that is sometimes 10 feet long. The resourceful owl deters predators by imitating the threatening buzz of a rattlesnake.

SEPTEMBER						
	1	2	3	4	5	
6	7	8	9	10	11	12
13	14	15	16	17	18	19
20	21	22	23	24	25	26
27	28	29	30			

eptember

6 Sunday

7 Monday
Labor Day

8 Tuesday

9 Wednesday

0 Thursday

1 Friday

2 Saturday

eated Woodpecker (*Dryocopus pileatus*). This crow-sized
lpecker—the largest of its kind in North America—is an uncommon resident
nse, mature forests throughout the northern and eastern regions of the con-
t. The pileated woodpecker is a "keystone" species, because its abandoned
holes are crucial for secondary users such as bufflehead and goldeneye ducks,
al and saw-whet owls, red squirrels and flying squirrels.

SEPTEMBER

		1	2	3	4	5
6	7	8	9	10	11	12
13	14	15	16	17	18	19
20	21	22	23	24	25	26
27	28	29	30			

eptember

3 Sunday

4 Monday

5 Tuesday

6 Wednesday

7 Thursday

8 Friday

9 Saturday

hinga (*Anhinga anhinga*). The anhinga is found in shallow inland , slow-moving rivers and swamps, from the southeastern United States to al South America. Two common names for the anhinga are "snakebird" and er." When swimming, the anhinga can adjust its buoyancy so that only its is visible above the water, giving it a snakelike appearance. When fishing, ird often uses its sharp, pointed bill as a harpoon to spear its meals.

SEPTEMBER

		1	2	3	4	5
6	7	8	9	10	11	12
13	14	15	16	17	18	19
20	21	22	23	24	25	26
27	28	29	30			

eptember

Bird Sightings

20 Sunday

21 Monday
First Day of Rosh Hashanah

22 Tuesday

23 Wednesday
Autumnal Equinox

24 Thursday

25 Friday

26 Saturday

rida Scrub Jay (*Aphelocoma coerulescens*). Found in scattered
es of scrub oak and palmetto palm throughout central Florida, the Florida
jay was elevated to a separate species, distinct from the western scrub jay
alifornica), in 1995. This jay has catholic tastes and eats everything from
s, insects and lizards to frogs, spiders and scorpions. Young Florida jays stay
heir parents for several years before they start families of their own.

SEPTEMBER

		1	2	3	4	5
6	7	8	9	10	11	12
13	14	15	16	17	18	19
20	21	22	23	24	25	26
27	28	29	30			

Bird Sightings

7 Sunday

8 Monday

9 Tuesday

0 Wednesday
Yom Kippur

1 Thursday

2 Friday

3 Saturday

SEPTEMBER

		1	2	3	4	5
6	7	8	9	10	11	12
13	14	15	16	17	18	19
20	21	22	23	24	25	26
27	28	29	30			

OCTOBER

					1	2	3
4	5	6	7	8	9	10
11	12	13	14	15	16	17
18	19	20	21	22	23	24
25	26	27	28	29	30	31

wn Booby (*Sula leucogaster*). A tropical seabird found throughout quatorial regions of the world, this brown booby was photographed in o's Sea of Cortez. Here, as in all other brown booby populations, the male emale exhibit identical physical characteristics. These birds catch fish by from as high as 90 feet, striking the water at speeds of up to 60 miles per A reinforced skull and air sacs beneath the skin cushion the impact.

)ctober

Bird Sightings

4 Sunday

5 Monday
Sukkoth

6 Tuesday

7 Wednesday

8 Thursday

9 Friday

0 Saturday

arlet Macaw (*Ara macao*). No other bird's beak can rival the power
at of a large parrot, such as the scarlet macaw. If it were necessary, this bird
l successfully cut through fence wire with its beak. In the wild, the scarlet
w uses its beak to break open the heavily armored seeds of tropical trees.
scarlet macaw lives in the dry deciduous forests and open woodlands of
al Central and South America.

OCTOBER						
				1	2	3
4	5	6	7	8	9	10
11	12	13	14	15	16	17
18	19	20	21	22	23	24
25	26	27	28	29	30	31

October

1 Sunday

2 Monday
Thanksgiving Day (Canada)
Columbus Day (U.S.)

3 Tuesday

4 Wednesday

5 Thursday

6 Friday

7 Saturday

illow Ptarmigan (*Lagopus lagopus*). The willow ptarmigan, one
e most widespread members of the grouse family, has a circumpolar range that
des arctic tundra areas in North America and tundra, moors and heathlands all
s Eurasia. This rusty-headed male is sporting his spring breeding plumage. In
er, both sexes in most ptarmigan populations turn white. As the bird's name
ests, the buds, leaves and flowers of willow plants are a mainstay of its diet.

OCTOBER						
				1	2	3
4	5	6	7	8	9	10
11	12	13	14	15	16	17
18	19	20	21	22	23	24
25	26	27	28	29	30	31

October

Bird Sightings

18 Sunday

19 Monday

20 Tuesday

21 Wednesday

22 Thursday

23 Friday

24 Saturday
Last Day of Daylight Saving Time

---

merican Black Oystercatcher (*Haematopus bachmani*).
chisel-shaped bill of the black oystercatcher is used to pry limpets and barna-
off rocks along the seashore, a diet that is supplemented by mussels and
ns. The bird wedges its bill between the two halves of the shell and severs the
scle that holds the shell closed. A bird of the Pacific Coast, the oystercatcher
ges from the Aleutian Islands of Alaska to Baja California.

OCTOBER						
				1	2	3
4	5	6	7	8	9	10
11	12	13	14	15	16	17
18	19	20	21	22	23	24
25	26	27	28	29	30	31

Bird Sightings

25 Sunday

26 Monday

27 Tuesday

28 Wednesday

29 Thursday

30 Friday

31 Saturday
Halloween

airie Falcon (*Falco mexicanus*). The fast-flying prairie falcon inhab-
he dry open grasslands, badlands and canyon country of the West, although
as been sighted as far east as Point Pelee, Ontario. The falcon preys on a wide
ety of songbirds, including meadowlarks, horned larks and mourning doves.
raptor usually snatches prey that is feeding on the ground or chases it in
nt, seizing it in midair.

OCTOBER						
				1	2	3
4	5	6	7	8	9	10
11	12	13	14	15	16	17
18	19	20	21	22	23	24
25	26	27	28	29	30	31

November

1 Sunday

2 Monday

3 Tuesday

4 Wednesday

5 Thursday

6 Friday

7 Saturday

red Grebe (*Podiceps nigricollis*). Unlike the solitary-nesting horned e, which is typically found one pair to a pond, the eared grebe breeds in e colonies that sometimes contain several hundred floating platform nests ioned from pond weeds. The eared grebe, identified by its short, slender bill, summer breeding bird on the freshwater lakes and sloughs of central North rica, Europe and southern Africa.

NOVEMBER						
1	2	3	4	5	6	7
8	9	10	11	12	13	14
15	16	17	18	19	20	21
22	23	24	25	26	27	28
29	30					

Bird Sightings

8 Sunday

9 Monday

0 Tuesday

1 Wednesday
Remembrance Day (Canada)
Veterans Day (U.S.)

2 Thursday

3 Friday

4 Saturday

ockhopper Penguin (*Eudyptes chrysocome*). The male rock-
per penguin guards his chicks constantly for the first three or four weeks
they emerge from the eggs. Although two rockhopper chicks often hatch,
second, smaller chick almost always dies. One of six different kinds of crested
guins, the rockhopper breeds on scattered island groups throughout the
hern Ocean. A seafood addict, it eats fish, krill and squid.

NOVEMBER						
1	2	3	4	5	6	7
8	9	10	11	12	13	14
15	16	17	18	19	20	21
22	23	24	25	26	27	28
29	30					

November

15 Sunday

16 Monday

17 Tuesday

18 Wednesday

19 Thursday

20 Friday

21 Saturday

---

d-Winged Blackbird (*Agelaius phoeniceus*). The scarlet
ɔlets of the male red-winged blackbird are a crucial adornment if the bird
defend a territory and attract a mate. When scientists blackened the red
ɔlder patches on a group of males, more than half immediately lost their ter-
ɔies to intruders. Found in wetlands throughout North America and Mexico,
redwing feeds on insects during the breeding season and seeds in winter.

NOVEMBER						
1	2	3	4	5	6	7
8	9	10	11	12	13	14
15	16	17	18	19	20	21
22	23	24	25	26	27	28
29	30					

November

22 Sunday

23 Monday

24 Tuesday

25 Wednesday

26 Thursday
Thanksgiving Day (U.S.)

27 Friday

28 Saturday

---

ack-Legged Kittiwake (*Rissa tridactyla*). A coastal bird of cir-
polar arctic waters, the loquacious black-legged kittiwake nests in cliff colonies
range in size from a few dozen birds to hundreds of thousands. The meager
es used by this bird demand that it build an elaborate nest to hold its eggs
ly. Its diet is the same as that of most seabirds of its kind—fish, crustaceans and
, which it picks from the water's surface as it swims.

NOVEMBER						
1	2	3	4	5	6	7
8	9	10	11	12	13	14
15	16	17	18	19	20	21
22	23	24	25	26	27	28
29	30					

November/December

29 Sunday

30 Monday

1 Tuesday

2 Wednesday

3 Thursday

4 Friday

5 Saturday

NOVEMBER

1	2	3	4	5	6	7
8	9	10	11	12	13	14
15	16	17	18	19	20	21
22	23	24	25	26	27	28
29	30					

:ller's Jay (*Cyanocitta stelleri*). In the mountains of western North :ica, the Steller's jay replaces the more familiar blue jay of the East. This jay amed after George Wilhelm Steller, a German naturalist who sailed with Vitus g in the North Pacific in the mid-1700s. During his travels, Steller described ssigned his name to a number of birds and mammals that were new to ce, including the jay, an eider, a sea lion and a sea cow that is now extinct.

DECEMBER

		1	2	3	4	5
6	7	8	9	10	11	12
13	14	15	16	17	18	19
20	21	22	23	24	25	26
27	28	29	30	31		

December

Bird Sightings

6 Sunday

7 Monday

8 Tuesday

9 Wednesday

0 Thursday

1 Friday

2 Saturday

rthern Hawk Owl (*Surnia ulula*). The northern hawk owl, here brooding three young owlets, is one of the few diurnal owls. It hunts ts, young hares, grouse and other birds in muskeg bogs and spruce forests s the entire breadth of the circumpolar boreal forest. It is also one of the wls that caches surplus food in trees, which enables it to survive lean times heavy snowfall makes prey more difficult to catch.

DECEMBER

		1	2	3	4	5
6	7	8	9	10	11	12
13	14	15	16	17	18	19
20	21	22	23	24	25	26
27	28	29	30	31		

December

3 Sunday

4 Monday
First Day of Chanukah

5 Tuesday

6 Wednesday

7 Thursday

8 Friday

9 Saturday

lantic Puffin (*Fratercula arctica*). Male and female Atlantic puffins dentical in physical appearance, and at the end of the breeding season, both me much duller-looking. They shed the blue-gray plate at the base of the bill, orange area fades, the yellow wattle at the corner of the mouth withers, the red ring disappears, and they lose their white faces. Puffins eat fish, crustaceans and ne worms, which they catch by "flying" underwater using their small, stiff wings.

DECEMBER

			1	2	3	4	5
6	7	8	9	10	11	12
13	14	15	16	17	18	19
20	21	22	23	24	25	26
27	28	29	30	31		

December

Bird Sightings

20 Sunday
_____

21 Monday
Winter Solstice
_____

22 Tuesday
_____

23 Wednesday
_____

24 Thursday
_____

25 Friday
Christmas Day
_____

26 Saturday
Boxing Day (Canada)
_____

iff Swallow (*Hirundo pyrrhonota*). Found in open country ughout North America, this house-building swallow fashions pellets of mud gourd-shaped nests that it cements to cliff walls. The bird has also adapted ructures in urban areas, placing its nests on the supports beneath bridges under the eaves of buildings. Colonies may contain more than 2,000 nests. all swallows, the fast-flying cliff swallow hunts for insects on the wing.

DECEMBER						
	1	2	3	4	5
6	7	8	9	10	11	12
13	14	15	16	17	18	19
20	21	22	23	24	25	26
27	28	29	30	31		

December/January

Bird Sightings

27 Sunday

28 Monday

29 Tuesday

30 Wednesday

31 Thursday

1 Friday
New Year's Day

2 Saturday

DECEMBER

		1	2	3	4	5
6	7	8	9	10	11	12
13	14	15	16	17	18	19
20	21	22	23	24	25	26
27	28	29	30	31		

d Phalarope (*Phalaropus fulicaria*). The elegant female red arope is larger and more brightly feathered than her mate. In a reversal of ler roles, the male takes on the tasks of incubating the eggs and caring for chicks. The phalarope nests in the circumpolar high Arctic and often feeds pinning rapidly on the surface of small tundra ponds, stirring up insects and crustaceans, which it then picks from the surface.

JANUARY 1999

					1	2
3	4	5	6	7	8	9
10	11	12	13	14	15	16
17	18	19	20	21	22	23
24/31	25	26	27	28	29	30

American Birding Association
Code of Ethic

We, the Membership of the American Birding Association, believe
that all birders have an obligation at all times to protect wildlife,
natural environment and the rights of others. We therefore pledge
ourselves to provide leadership in meeting this obligation by adher
to the following general guidelines of good birding behavior.

I. Birders must always act in ways that do not endanger the welfare of birds or other wildlife.

In keeping with this principle, we will
• Observe and photograph birds without knowingly disturbin
them in any significant way.
• Avoid chasing or repeatedly flushing birds.
• Only sparingly use recordings and similar methods of attract
ing birds and not use these methods in heavily birded areas.
• Keep an appropriate distance from nests and nesting colonie
so as not to disturb them or expose them to danger.
• Refrain from handling birds or eggs unless engaged in recog-
nized research activities.

II. Birders must always act in ways that do not harm the natural environment.

In keeping with this principle, we will
• Stay on existing roads, trails and pathways whenever possible
to avoid trampling or otherwise disturbing fragile habitat.
• Leave all habitat as we found it.

III. Birders must always respect the rights of others.

In keeping with this principle, we will
• Respect the privacy and property of others by observing
"No Trespassing" signs and by asking permission to enter priv
or posted lands.
• Observe all laws and the rules and regulations which govern
public use of birding areas.
• Practice common courtesy in our contact with others. For
example, we will limit our requests for information, and we w
make them at reasonable hours of the day.
• Always behave in a manner that will enhance the image of th
birding community in the eyes of the public.

Birders in groups should assume special responsibilities.

roup members, we will
ke special care to alleviate the problems and disturbances
are multiplied when more people are present.
t in consideration of the group's interest, as well as our own.
pport by our actions the responsibility of the group leader(s)
the conduct of the group.

roup leaders, we will
sume responsibility for the conduct of the group.
arn and inform the group of any special rules, regulations or
duct applicable to the area or habitat being visited.
mit groups to a size that does not threaten the environment
he peace and tranquillity of others.
ach others birding ethics by our words and example.

rtesy of the American Birding Association

he Photographer

Dr. Wayne Lynch is Canada's best-known and most widely published professional wildlife photographer, the author of award-winning books and television documentaries and a popular guest lecturer. His photo credits include hundreds of magazine covers, thousands of calendar shots and tens of thousands of images published in over 30 countries.

Lynch, who lives in Calgary, Alberta, with his wife Aubrey Lang, is also the
or of *Bears, Bears, Bears* and *A is for Arctic: Natural Wonders
Polar World*, both published by Firefly Books.